2008
Autumn.

storage
solutions

margaret sabo wills

METRO BOOKS
NEW YORK

WELDON OWEN GROUP
Chief Executive Officer **John Owen**
Chief Financial Officer **Simon Fraser**

WELDON OWEN INC.
Chief Executive Officer and President **Terry Newell**
Senior VP, International Sales **Stuart Laurence**
VP, Sales and Marketing **Amy Kaneko**

VP, Creative Director **Gaye Allen**
Senior Art Director **Emma Boys**
Designers **Diana Heom** and **Anna Giladi**

VP, Publisher **Roger Shaw**
Executive Editor **Elizabeth Dougherty**
Managing Editor **Karen Templer**
Project Editor **Veronica Peterson**
Editorial Assistant **Sarah Gurman**

Production Director **Chris Hemesath**
Production Manager **Michelle Duggan**
Color Manager **Teri Bell**

A WELDON OWEN PRODUCTION
Copyright © 2008 Weldon Owen Inc.

Metro Books
122 Fifth Avenue
New York, NY 10011

ISBN-13: 978-1-4351-0756-4
ISBN-10: 1-4351-0756-X

Printed in China

10 9 8 7 6 5 4 3 2 1

contents

the organized life

Back in the overstuffed Victorian era, William Morris counseled, "Have nothing in your houses that you do not know to be useful, or believe to be beautiful." He said nothing about how best to store the belongings that meet that standard, but it remains a good guiding principle in our own time of abundance.

So what do we do with it all? Storage problems are the result of clutter—an excess of stuff. Storage solutions begin with separating the trash from the treasures. If you blanch at the idea of decluttering a whole house, take it one room (or even one drawer) at a time. Arm yourself with four containers—trash, recycle, give away, and store—and then scrutinize each item. If you don't use it but someone else could, pass it along, but you might be surprised at how much you discard. As you go, remind yourself that gifts require a warm thank-you, not necessarily a lifelong home; that you needn't always keep an object to hang on to the memory it represents; and that, without all the clutter, prized possessions will have greater presence.

After the streamlining, assess what's left. The key to organization is to group like things. In the kitchen, we put flatware in one drawer, dish towels in another. Use this same approach throughout the house. When you've sorted out your belts, scarves, and necklaces, or your brushes, paints, and hand tools, you can start to see what sorts (and sizes) of shelves, cabinets, or containers each group will require—and to think about which oft-used tools or favored objects you'll want out in the open, and which you'd prefer to stow away.

Finding just the right place for every last thing will take some determination and a little creativity, but at this point you're already headed toward a more organized and efficient life. Let William Morris's words and this book be your guide.

living

There's no getting around it: life equals stuff. But when you strike the right balance between closed storage and artful display, that stuff is what gives a room life. Put your best belongings on open shelves and stow more mundane things in drawers or behind doors.

geared for daily life

It takes only one individual to create a storage calamity, but the more people there are in a given household, the greater the challenge of keeping your living space tidy.

shelve it

Shelving is an essential item, but it can be as simple as boards on milk crates or as elaborate as custom built-ins. Explore the wide range of styles now available for every budget, and plan to use your shelves for far more than just books.

multitask

Choose furniture that earns its floor space by doubling as storage: a coffee table with drawers; a lidded ottoman; a room divider of open shelving; or a wall unit configured for books, a television, a stereo, and all of the corresponding media.

seek trouble

Note which spots are magnets for household flotsam and address them accordingly. If newly arrived magazines get strewn all over the house, appoint a shelf for them. If shoes pile up by a couch, place a sturdy basket nearby.

give cues

Keep things categorized and in logical places, and don't be shy about labels and dictums. The more clearly you are able to convey where every last thing goes, the more likely the whole family will be to stick with whatever system you've created.

contain it

Container stores sell boxes and bins for every conceivable purpose, in a wide range of styles, but you'll also want to scout out idiosyncratic options. Look for old footlockers, blanket chests, retail display cases, or milk cans, for instance.

go vertical

Maximize storage with furniture that uses height for extra capacity, such as a wall-mounted shelf or cabinet in an otherwise unused spot. Activate the space above doors by running a single shelf around a whole room, just below the ceiling.

the family library

Books are at their very tidiest—and thus better companions for a mix of objects—when lined up along their spines. Book stands display treasured volumes.

mixed media Since DVDs, CDs, tapes, and records come in uniform sizes, they slip neatly into shelves of corresponding heights, either with or without doors.

made for tv

Media cabinetry can be designed to hide the television or to highlight it. In either case, keep remotes under control by designating a caddy.

framing device Just as matching frames can unify an assortment of pictures, bookcases can tie together disparate contents—whether extra pillows or a television.

the best storage is that which leaves room for character

Books have a way of mounting up, which is part of their charm for many readers. These gleaming metal shelves provide a framework for a collection, but without forcing it into regimented rows. The shelves are deep enough to accommodate oversized art volumes or doubled stacks of smaller books.

let the sun shine in

Allowing space for generous
windows, a harmonious band
of low shelving holds books
and magazines, continuing as
drawers under a window seat.
Matching shelves across the
room support a large mirror.

in plain sight In a hallway (above), floor-to-ceiling ledges face art books forward. Artworks on wide moldings (right) swap out easily with new acquisitions.

woodpile redux

For uninterrupted
fireside evenings,
store logs nearby—in
a framed-out niche,
stacked tidily under
the hearth ledge, or
in a sturdy tub or pot.

go wide A low, rough-planked cabinet spans this room, serving as both display ledge and catchall, while blending into the equally rugged post-and-beam interior.

setting boundaries See-through metal toy shelves delineate a play nook in this sleek living room. Similar chrome shelving does heavier duty in both spaces.

workspace

Whether you're working, spending time online, or enjoying a favorite hobby, configuring a dedicated space for your chosen pursuit makes it easier to get down to business. The key to a workspace you'll love: storage specifically tailored to your task.

equipped for the job

The greatest benefit of having a tailored workspace is the luxury of focus—you won't be constantly breaking your concentration to hunt down what you need.

be particular

Ensure that your personal workspace needs are addressed by first sorting out what they are. Is your challenge to corral craft supplies, keep tools on view, store big artworks, or manage paperwork? List your concerns and find a solution for each.

prioritize

Make the worktable or desk your command center: keep your most frequently used items within reach and stow everything else out of the way. Archives, records, and anything rarely accessed might go into another space entirely.

make space

Desks, shelving, file cabinets, and dividers can define an office within any open area, giving it both privacy and credence. Built-in desks and shelving maximize the space; freestanding pieces offer flexibility as your space needs evolve.

think small

Whether buttons and threads, tubes of paint, or disks and manuals, small things can be vital to your work. Arrange like things into groups and store them in appropriately sized containers, divided drawers, slotted shelves, or labeled file folders.

know your style

If you crave a calm and austere workspace, you'll need ample drawers and cabinets. If, on the other hand, you feel inspired when surrounded by meaningful piles of stuff, go for bulletin boards, open shelves, and lots of available counter space.

store safely

Will you be sharing office space with a toddler or a pet? If so, conceal power cords in plastic casing and stow away any hazardous materials and tools. Anchor top-heavy bookcases, and be careful not to overload any wall-hung shelves.

new definition At one end of an open loft, vintage credenzas and an antique desk conjure up a fully formed office, with a mix of open and closed storage.

labeled for use

Buckets labeled with colorful copies of their contents, supplies in clear bins, and cleverly marked file drawers make it easy to locate whatever you need.

work styles

Shelves and cabinets hung on
wall-mounted brackets (left)
form a hardworking backdrop
for a bright, streamlined desk.
Quieter neutrals (above) allow
a household command center
to blend into the kitchen.

found space Offices can fit gracefully into unused nooks–in an under-stair alcove or on a landing. Shelving and matched boxes keep clutter under control.

behind closed doors With a laptop and ample vertical storage, even a closet can hold a compact office. And closet doors hide it away quickly and easily.

neutral space

A simple board on brackets and a patch of grass cloth form a quiet office in a bedroom corner. Clipboards, a modified clothesline, and stacks of cigar boxes bring order to the mix of things on and over the desk.

under the eaves

To make way for work, this attic's contents were boxed up, numbered, and inventoried. Blueprint drawers and a factory table provide flat storage and a desk.

ready for work

Storage-rich tables, a wall
of tools, large cabinets, and
a built-in desk add up to a
multipurpose workroom.

room to create

The focus of this family-friendly room is the worktable—its shelves, drawers, and bins brimming with the stuff of art. In/out baskets for the kids keep things in order. At the desk (left), an elevated Plexiglas surface keeps tools on view and at hand.

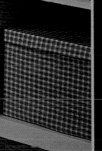

sew inspired

Clear jars and labeled
boxes organize trim,
buttons, scraps, and
thread. Ribbon spools
are threaded on a rod,
handy for sewing and
gift wrapping alike.

skein scheme Lucky for avid practitioners of the fiber arts, the requisite yarns and needles store beautifully out in the open, adding up to a richly textured display.

kitchens

Nowhere in the home are storage concerns more intensive than in the kitchen, where standard banks of cabinetry are only the start. To make sure there is truly a place for everything—from skillets to spices, teacups to towels—you'll need to think outside the built-in box.

configured for cooks

No matter the size or style of your kitchen, getting it in order and keeping it that way hinges on everyone who uses the space knowing exactly what goes where.

be motion-minded

Observe how you use your kitchen to pinpoint organizational needs. Do you find you have to cross the room multiple times to accomplish any given task? If so, try to consolidate things used together near the point at which they're used.

think logically

Follow the golden rule of kitchen storage: place things near the fixture or appliance they relate to. Glasses should be next to the fridge, dish towels and soaps near the sink, pots and pans by the stove. Keep extra trash bags in the bottom of the can.

ask for proof

Reserve the most easily accessed areas—the countertops and those cabinets between waist and eye level—for the things you use most. Relegate holiday platters and other rarely used pieces to harder-to-reach spots, either high or low.

max out cabinets

With shelves too deep or too far apart, much of a cabinet's capacity can be wasted. Bring every inch into service with stacking risers, slide-out bins on rails, vertical dividers, and lazy Susans. Wherever possible, attach racks and hooks to doors.

use displays

The stuff of hospitality— from condiment bottles and serving platters to table linens and fine china—humanizes the atmosphere of a working kitchen. Consider storing these in the open, but be sure to keep them away from smoke and grease.

catch strays

Many kitchen storage challenges have nothing to do with the culinary arts. Set up permanent spots or even temporary holding zones for books, schoolbags, papers, toys, and anything else that tends to collect on the kitchen table or counters.

everything at hand Rods with S-hooks make a pot rack that much handier.
Over an island, a suspended shelf keeps oils, preserves, and seasonings in reach.

64

daily display

Behind an oft-used range (left), oils line up on a ledge over utensil rails. Dish towels and root vegetables are stashed in large bowls beneath the island. When kept on display, collections of practical items (above and right) can be both used and admired.

hidden assets

Running floor to ceiling and
wall to wall, these smooth
laminate cabinets offer an
enviable amount of storage.
Strategically placed niches
break up the expanse and
showcase collectibles.

rough ideas

Fruit crates tucked into doorless base cabinets increase this kitchen's utility—and its rustic appeal.

a stealth kitchen A silver tea service, glassware, and brown pottery form quiet displays above base cabinets so elegant in design that they appear to be furniture.

attractive opposites A ceiling-height hutch demarcates an open kitchen. The wooden hutch and table stand in charming contrast to the stainless-steel cabinetry.

a new view

In this 100-year-old brick building, once the town library, shelves now hold dining-room necessities, with vertical slots housing platters, cutting boards, rolled linens, and wines.

objects of attention This kitchen's compact core, with tiny upper cabinets, is an unobtrusive backdrop for shelves of colorful collectibles at the front of the space.

company ready

A party's worth of dishes
and linens demands a lot of
storage. Luckily, such things
exude hospitality, whether
stored in a sleekly modern
hallway pantry or piled in a
weathered antique hutch.

a decor dictum

Nearly everything is beautiful in multiples, here demonstrated by simple spice tins (left) and oils and vinegars massed in an antique toolbox (above). On "floating" shelves (right), groups of tin cups, canisters, and coffee presses mingle with nature prints.

store and protect

Stow wine on its side not just for good looks and space savings, but to keep the corks from drying out. To prolong the wine's life, keep temperatures steady.

bathrooms

Though they're traditionally among the smallest rooms in a house, bathrooms can make big storage demands. Use space-smart strategies to marshal all the toiletries, bath towels, medicines, and cosmetics, and you'll soon be beginning (and ending) your day in organized bliss.

prepared for action

Bathroom storage often must accommodate multiple people—frequently during the most hectic times of the day—in a space that has a high potential for clutter.

see the needs

Consider the role of the space. A powder room, for example, might need to hold only extra toilet paper and hand towels for guests, while a family bath must handle multiple family members and their towels and toiletries on a day-in, day-out basis.

conquer clutter

Scout out eye-catching containers to organize necessary gear, both on countertops and in the depths of the vanity. Trays or bins of related items not only keep things orderly but can also be pulled out as needed, then restowed.

ward off water

Bathroom furnishings and any open displays must contend with the splashing of water and general dampness that are characteristic of the space. Store dry towels where they'll stay fresh, and put tub toys where they can fully dry out.

think safety

Given a bathroom's often tight dimensions and wet surfaces, plan storage so that everyone can grasp what they need without any precarious reaching or climbing. Always keep electrical items, such as blow-dryers and curling irons, away from water.

waste no space

Take full advantage of vertical space with hooks high on walls and on the backs of doors, and with shelving or a cabinet over the toilet. Store items used less often in higher spots and, for reaching them safely, provide a slip-resistant step stool.

rethink built-ins

A freestanding chest or bureau can be a stylish addition to a bathroom's built-ins while adding storage capacity. Sinks can be mounted in or on many types of furniture, so consider replacing a drab vanity with a vintage chest, cabinet, or table.

custom built

Built-ins abound in this spacious his-and-hers bath, where a tub-side vanity table leads to a dressing alcove with towel shelves and a lidded storage bench.

warming trends

Wall-hung drawers (above) and doors of richly figured wood (right) conceal storage space in these contemporary bathrooms. The absence of shiny knobs downplays the cabinetry's utilitarian nature.

furnished for function Freestanding furniture pieces add style and storage capacity to any bathroom, but especially those lacking built-in vanities or cabinets.

the little things

No need to hide the cotton swabs and washcloths—remove necessities from their packaging and group everything in cups, trolleys, jars, or trays.

geometric proof Geometry conveys order, as demonstrated by the neat grids of built-in niches (left) and of stacked boxes punctuated by toilet-paper circles.

towel off

Sleek, newer vanities (left) substitute towel bars for drawers. A weathered towel rack (above) lends age and texture to a room. Folded and stacked in a glass-fronted cabinet (right), bath towels are integral to the room's maritime color scheme.

maximized for capacity

Get the infrastructure of your closet right—whether it's designed to hold clothing, linens, or supplies—and you'll find it easy to organize the contents and maintain order.

use every inch

Increase the capacity of an insufficient closet by reconfiguring or adding to the available shelves, drawers, and rods. Hang shirts and pants on tiered rods, installing the lower one 42 inches from the floor, and the upper 36 inches above that.

think extras

Inventory the nonclothes aspects of your wardrobe and tabulate the storage you'll need for jewelry, scarves, belts, neckties, and shoes. Boxes can hold off-season clothing, while hooks on doors receive jackets, pajamas, or tomorrow's outfit.

light it up

Make the darker parts of your closet more visibly accessible by having a simple light installed. If an electrician is beyond your budget, look for stick-on battery-powered lights. Glossy white paint on the interior walls will make everything easier to see.

invent space

If your dresser isn't doing its fair share of clothes containment, frame in an extra closet instead—or enclose an alcove with folding doors. For a less labor-intensive approach, mount racks and rods in a corner and use a curtain or floor screen for cover.

shop for help

Tap services for custom closets, or check out any home-improvement or organizational store for modular prefabricated systems in laminate, fine wood, or coated wire. Either approach can be used to create a closet or augment an existing one.

be generous

In hanging clothes, leave room for air to circulate, and allow enough space on the rods to remove an item without thoroughly rumpling its neighbors. Figure 1 to 2 inches from one shirt hanger to the next, and 2 inches for pant and skirt hangers.

personal space A low dresser and a simple wall of built-in clothes storage turn an awkward space under a roofline into a charming and efficient dressing room.

island of calm

More luxurious than
a walk-in closet is a
walk-around dressing
room, where rods and
drawers are just the
beginning. Trays in
various sizes, lined up
on shelves, keep
accessories sorted.
Out-of-season items
are safely stowed in
lidded, labeled boxes.

newly configured

A standard closet becomes as capacious as a walk-in when it's fully partitioned into easy-to-scan compartments.

sorting it out Whether in a glass-doored walk-in or a pullout trolley, the key to high-functioning clothes storage is to sort everything by color, size, and type.

clever disguise

Folding doors enclose an alcove to create a closet. Coats slip discreetly behind a false wall. Papered to match, both closets blend into the walls.

smart steps Put the space beneath stairs to work with shoes slipped onto shelves behind the risers (above) or with rolling trundles in graduated sizes (right).

let's get dressed

A rod and curtains in front of a built-in hutch result in a spacious closet (left). Graphic icons (above and right) help kids sort their own clothes and shoes.

beyond the built-in A tent of creamy fabric and a curtain tie-back turn an empty corner into a closet; a row of peak-roofed lockers evokes seaside cabanas.

second life

A deep picture frame acts as a shadow box for a family photo and heirloom jewels (left). Petri dishes and an antique cigarette tin (above and right) make surprisingly smart jewelry storage, separating chains and delicate pieces.

linen closet reinvented

A trolley on casters (above)
keeps stacks of folded sheets
handy beneath a platform bed.
An antique iron crib frame
(right) displays a colorful
collection of rolled quilts.

utility rooms

Rain gear, laundry supplies, sports equipment, garden tools—crucial elements of any household, but far from glamorous. To corral these things while keeping them accessible is the challenge of a utility room. Get it right and your household will run more smoothly than ever.

designed for use

Laundry rooms, mudrooms, utility spaces, and supply closets are all meant to be behind-the-scenes aids in keeping a household running smoothly.

ease routines

In your mind or in reality, take a walk through the daily comings and goings of your family. Then plan suitable spots within entryways or hallways for everything you encounter along the route—from car keys and umbrellas to baseballs and backpacks.

get hooked

If your home doesn't have a mudroom, mount a row of hooks along a wall near the main door, add a bench if space permits, and line up shoes below. This provides a place to keep outerware tidy and accessible and a space for wet items to dry.

gather forces

Housekeeping tasks are inherently foreseeable and repetitive, which makes it a relatively easy exercise to collect all the tools and supplies for a given chore into a handy location. There they will be reliably waiting to be called into service.

grab and go

Often, a utility room is a staging area for supplies and tools to be used in other parts of the house. For maximum efficiency, line a shelf or cabinet with caddies equipped for basic housecleaning, small repair work, and garden maintenance.

iron it out

If you prefer to iron in a bedroom or the kitchen instead of in the laundry room, configure a nearby closet to accommodate the ironing board and other necessities, rather than storing them in the laundry room and hauling them back and forth.

borrow space

Garages often contain wasted space. Carve a potting room out of one end with a standard base cabinet and overhead shelves, or install ample cabinetry and turn the entire garage into a mixed-use workshop the whole family can enjoy.

a proper greeting

Below hooks for hats and coats, a generous sideboard, baskets, boot cubbies, and a pair of umbrella stands meet whatever comes through the front door.

mudless mudroom Hooks and racks corral everything from brooms to boots.
Wall-mounted cubbies, lined with mats, make room for a built-in dog bed.

all in the family

In a cloakroom for the whole crew, personalized lockers, assorted bins, and a rack for book bags coordinate today's comings and tomorrow's goings. Chalkboards turn the space into a message center.

new laundry outlook

This spacious laundry
room boasts folding space,
a rolling hamper, and
overhead shelves. Sprays
and soaps stored in pretty
bottles and canisters make
the job feel less like a chore.

a supply surprise Bright floral prints add whimsy to a household supply closet sensibly outfitted with lined wicker baskets and convenient fabric catchalls.

pegged a winner Simple-to-install Peg-Board is as useful for toys as tools. Baskets of additional equipment are easily transported to the backyard or ball field.

fertile ideas

Rows of deep drawers and
wide shelves–lined with flats,
canisters, and bins–keep this
potting shed organized.